MW01365981

in September and Other Poems

Other works published by the author, available from iUniverse:

The Longest Month and Other Poems (2016)
An Apology and Other Poems (2016)
A Bell Curve and Other Poems (2013)
An Artist's Model and Other Poems (2012)
Black Hole and Other Poems (2012)
Pursuit and Other Poems (2011)
Persistence and Other Poems (2010)
Celebrations and Other Poems (2009)
War-Wise and Other Poems (2009)
Surface Tension and Other Poems (2008)
Confusion Matrix and Other Poems (2007)

Summer in September and Other Poems

David J. Murray

SUMMER IN SEPTEMBER AND OTHER POEMS

iUniverse books may be ordered through booksellers or by contacting:

iUniverse
1663 Liberty Drive
Bloomington, IN 47403
www.iuniverse.com
1-800-Authors (1-800-288-4677)

ISBN: 978-1-4917-9224-7 (sc)
ISBN: 978-1-4917-9225-4 (hc)
ISBN: 978-1-4917-9226-1 (e)

Print information available on the last page.

iUniverse rev. date: 6/2/2016

Contents

Blue Mountain Resort

Praise Poems

Sleep Poems

Introduction

In my previous volume, *The Longest Month and Other Poems*, I described how, at the end of May 2015, I met a recently widowed friend of long standing at a train station. We spent the period of June to September visiting each other (me in a Toronto high rise with a view of Lake Ontario, she in the countryside in the French-speaking province of Quebec) and occasionally taking side trips.

It so happened that September 2015 was the warmest September in the 136 years during which weather records had been kept for the Toronto area. All the poems in the present volume were written between June and September 2015, so the whole set was titled *Summer in September and Other Poems*. Many of these were seen and commented on by my friend; the changes made as a result of her suggestions were agreed by both of us to be improvements on my original versions.

This interaction took an unexpected turn when she began to write her own poems in response to some of my individual poems. In this volume, these paired poems, one by me and one by her, have been printed adjacently. For convenience in showing who wrote which poem, my poems are printed in normal type, and hers are prefaced by SHE. In the present volume, the 90 poems have been divided into ten sections. All the paired poems will be found in Section 5.

Section 1 ("In Memoriam") includes only two poems. The first is dedicated to her deceased husband, whose ashes lie under a newly planted oak tree in a heritage site near their Quebec home. The second is dedicated to my deceased wife, Esther, whose ashes lie in a gravesite in the Cataraqui Cemetery in Kingston, Ontario. Section 2 ("Travelling") begins with the eponymous "Summer in September" and contains five poems about how I felt when I met my friend off a bus or a train on our various visits. Section 3 ("My Place") contains five poems about her visits to me, and Section 4 ("Your Place") has five poems about my visits to her, where we were surrounded by farmland, and where a car is a necessity to get from one place to another, including local farmers' markets with superb selections of local cheeses, charcuterie and vegetables.

Section 5 ("Phone Calls and Letters") starts with a poem about how much I enjoyed hearing her voice during our many long-distance phone conversations. Twelve paired poems are then presented.

Section 6 ("The Great Wolf Lodge") includes five poems I wrote, in her absence, at the Great Wolf Lodge in Niagara Falls, Canada, where my two children and four grandchildren joined me for a short holiday. I then travelled to join my friend in Montreal, with a side trip to Kingston to view Esther's grave; I wrote six poems during this visit, and they're included in Section 7 ("Montreal and Kingston"). Section 8 ("Blue Mountain Resort") includes three poems written when we both attended the wedding of one of my former students, Christina Bandomir, which was held at the Blue Mountain Lodge, near the edge of Lake Huron, in the middle of September 2015.

Section 9 ("Praise Poems") includes 20 poems, the second of which ("Endnote #2") includes a question first asked in my earlier *Persistence and Other Poems*, on page 42. All the poems in Section 9 are presented in the chronological order. Section 10 ("Sleep Poems") includes 13 poems; the last, "Thousands," was one of my friend's personal favourites.

I am indebted, again, to Arnie Fernandez of iUniverse for her assistance with preparing my handwritten text for publication. I am once again indebted to Rachel Breau, MLIS, for research assistance. My friend and I particularly want to thank Christina Bandomir and Paul Gallivan for inviting us to their splendid wedding. Needless to say, my gratitude to my friend is boundless for her help with improving, and refreshingly supplementing, some of my poems.

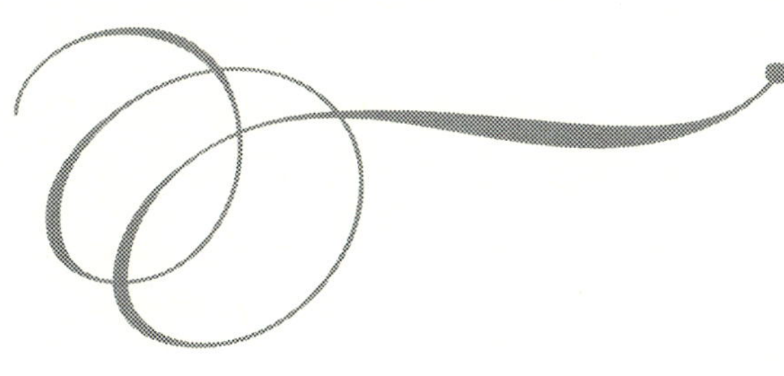

In Memoriam

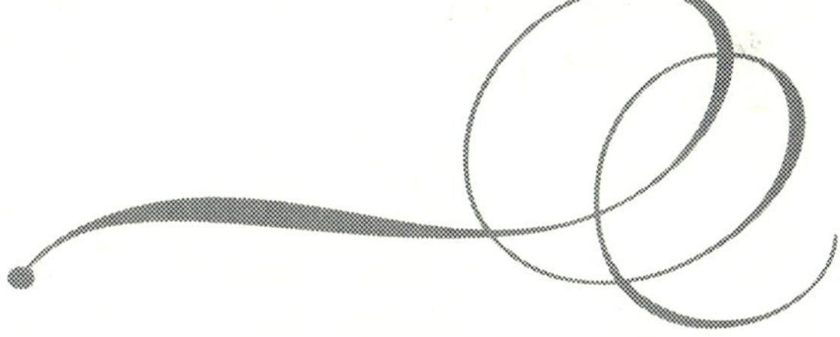

Beneath an Oak

This is an earth where he can always rest,
Released from earthly fortunes and from strife.
He's disengaged from these and need no longer
Deal with the feats and fictions of his life.

He'd lain in arms that spoke her loving to him.
Sometimes he'd piloted to other skies,
But now he's forever grounded, and their love has
Consecrated the ground in which he lies.

Upon an Oak

On a summer afternoon we spotted a bird
Larger than any I'd ever seen before
On that sunlit hillside, where our Esther lies
But never hears the birdsong anymore.

You wondered if perhaps it was a hawk
That sat so sedately, peering into the still
Of that summer sunlight from the silent oak
On which it sat in solitude, until

Downward it flew, a flash of brown and white
And terracotta in its elegance.
That red-tailed hawk transfixed us at its sight,
But Esther would never see its brilliance.

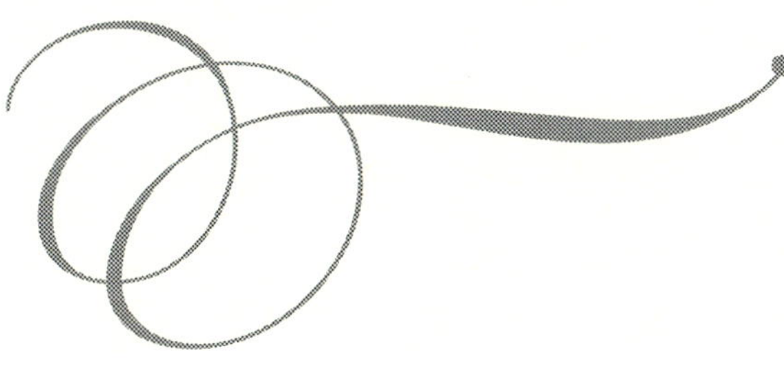

Travelling

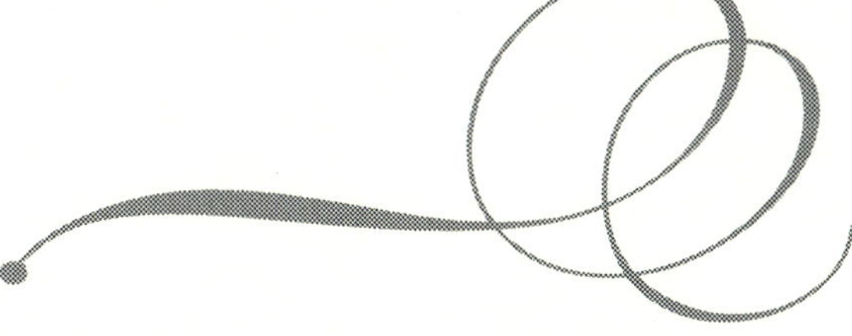

Summer in September

If every day brought a sunset
Like the one I saw tonight,
Where scudding lines criss-crossed the sky
With yellow-brown and red and white,
Then I could show you what I'd meant
By "summer in September."
But the sunset went.

If every day a steady light
Were thrust across the blue
Left by a day whose summer's heat
Had riddled my thoughtscape through and through,
Then I could say what I'd intended
By "summer in September."
But the sunset ended.

And if, every day, the evening sky
Were slotted with sunny rays
That etched a promise that tomorrow
Would bring the sunniest of days,
Then I could give my opinion
Of "summer in September."
But the sunset's gone.

But tomorrow, when you finally arrive
And step from the train to the ground,
To where I've been waiting impatiently
For the distant whistle and the engine's sound,
I'll know that summer cannot disappear
Because you'll bring it with you while you're here.

When You Step off the Train

If rain should blot and scar the next few days
Before your magic self steps off the train,
I shall be quite at rest and take my ease;
The weather will chase those showers away again.

But if it be sunny, warm, and the air is mild,
Then darken over, blotting out the sky,
I shall wax wroth like an irritated child,
Because it might teem with rain as the days roll by.

But if it should be weatherless and grey
When you step down from the highness of the car,
Then I'll monumentalize that day
As the one when you stepped, just like a movie star,

Onto the long grey platform of the station
Where, star-struck, I stood fixed in adulation.

When You Meet Me at the Station

I do not count the days until your hair
And idyllic self appear to me for real,
Unfantasized, and standing at a spot
In a busy city station where—alas!—
There is no surging cloud of steam or scream
Of howling whistle like the express train
That scales the opening of *Brief Encounter.*
Here are just people, voices, and, yes, you
In radiant yesness waiting there for me.

I live the days until your silhouette,
Idyllic and sylph-like, next appears to me
Amidst the crowd of scurrying, eager feet
That patter through the station's promenade,
All heading somewhere other than the station.
But you stay at your spot, magnificent
Fusion of everything I've ever sought,
Standing there for real, unfantasized,
Knowing I will burst with adoration.

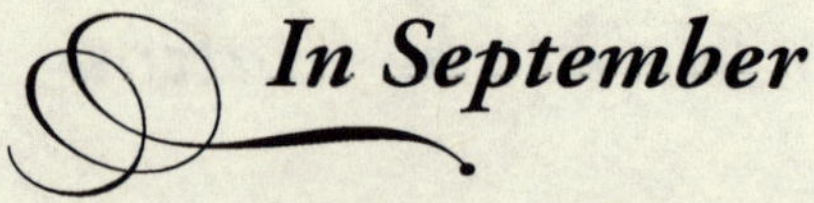

In September

Once again the first pale red
Redecorates the scene
As autumn steals from each tree's head
Its verdant summer's green.

But I think of you this fall, instead
Of problems that endure.
My recent autumns all have led
To searches for their cure.

But your presence here will render them dead,
The weariness of the past.
You will be here while the tall trees shed
Colours that cannot last.

And you will be here when the fall has fled
And settle winter's score,
Drowning its radical cold and dread
More than I've known before.

On My Way to You

Perhaps I am too arrogant if I assert
That you will beckon me when I am on my path
Of yearning, on my way to meet entrancing you
(Provided I do not bring you viruses for a cold).

Perhaps I am too bold if I state it over-baldly
That you are the be-all and end-all, finale, and ultimate-all
Of the path, unflowered, of buses, trains and taxicabs
I ride to greet you (but not too effusively in public).

Perhaps I am too clinging if I dare to claim,
After battling with a crossword on the moving train
As it surged through the leafy whizzed-by trees, that nonetheless
You were always in my mind (for you mustn't think I'm obsessed).

And neither is this a final couplet claiming closure;
There hardly seems an end to my wordy self-exposure.

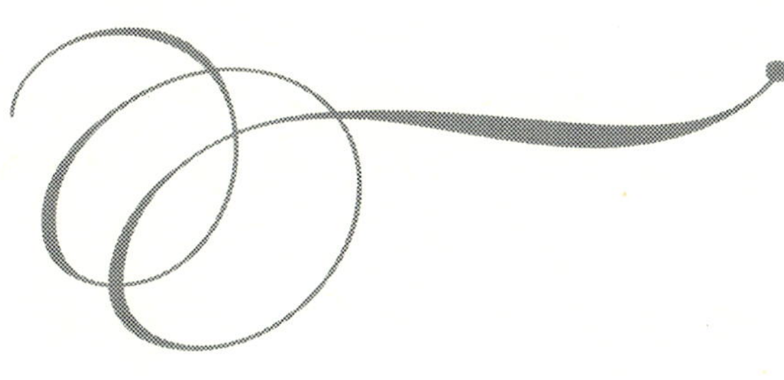

My Place

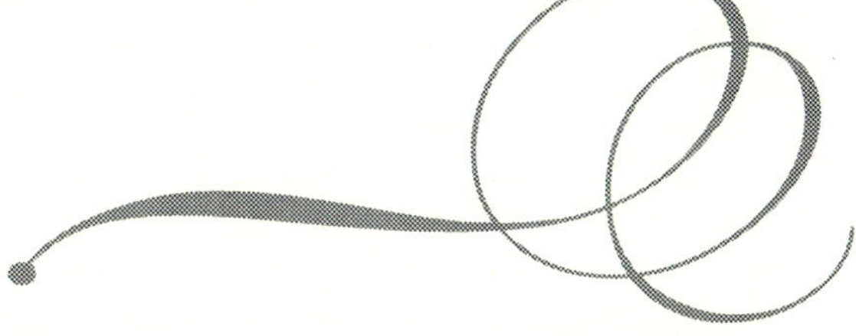

A Dawning Truth

A slow suspicion, then the dawning truth:
Those seeming spurs of broken grey and brown,
Stiff-standing tree trunks bearing empty branches;
Those mist-like blots upon the speckled hill,
Brown islands in an ocean of green trees,

Are dead. The emerald ash borer—a name
That dares to thrust itself upon this verse,
So smoothly do its syllables combine
In memory—has literally bored
Those ash trees to a dull arboreal death.

From here, or more precisely, far away,
I image your effervescent, lively self,
With life itself evolving from your presence,
And I search therein for death so that I can
Compare it with nature visible here—but I can't.

Now Comes Cold

Now spills great lucre from a stainless sky,
Turning the lake to a stream of steely grey
In preparation for a rainy day.

I heard the winds grow louder, blustering
At how they're coming closer with their wet
And daunting raindrops falling closer yet.

So far, sunshine has drenched our holiday.
But now comes cold, and blistering autumn's fall,
With a whistling wind that pounds against it all,

And an outward foray onto my balcony,
Buttoned and behatted though I was,
Was followed by retreat indoors because

I had to find a pen and paper quickly.
Nature herself had made me blind
When she thrust that opening line upon my mind.

Surfacing

Socializing here, alone, was fun,
But I've been impatient to have it over and done
And let my undermind, obsessed with you,
Surface at last, lucid, untrammeled and true,
Until it vies with the hillscape I see here
In producing sonic colours, pure and clear.

Looking forward to Your Cooking

I greet this evening's dusk with gratitude.
It's close to seven and by this time next week,
The clock will have its sullen hands at six,
And what is dusk today be darkness then.

But in days, not weeks, I'll end my solitude.
With you will I be then, and your unique,
Delectable warm hearth will provide its mix
Of unbelievable *gourmandise* again.

And I know already that, diced crude
But ravishingly mingling with leek,
Butts and ends of aubergines will fix
Perfection into stuffings that will span

A mushroom's open cavity and make
My future bachelor's mealtimes hard to take.

Moonlight

Night falls, and its blackened fingers scrape the tops
Of trees to a moonlit glare.
A string of yips reveals coyotes hunting
Innocently there.
The woody reed tops brush the silent wind
Into something shadowy.
The clouds move quickly, high across the sky,
Moonlit and billowy.
The road sends asphalt gleams where moonlight falls
To whiten its tones;
The roof you're under softens to a sigh
A night-wind's groans.
Envious, I dislodge, with a long-distance finger,
A hair from your sleeping brow,
And I look at you under the long-distance moonlight
And wish I were with you now.

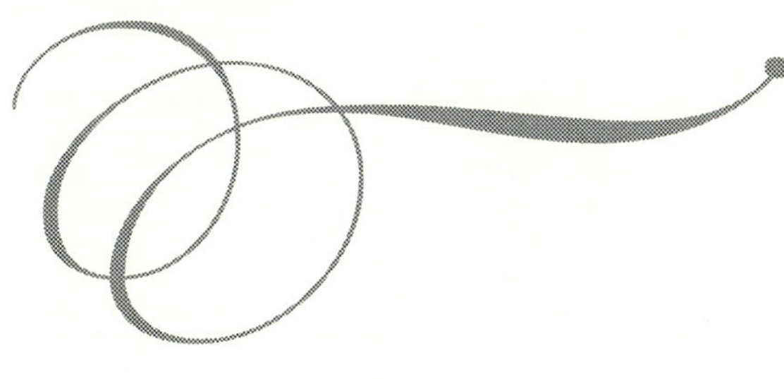

Your Place

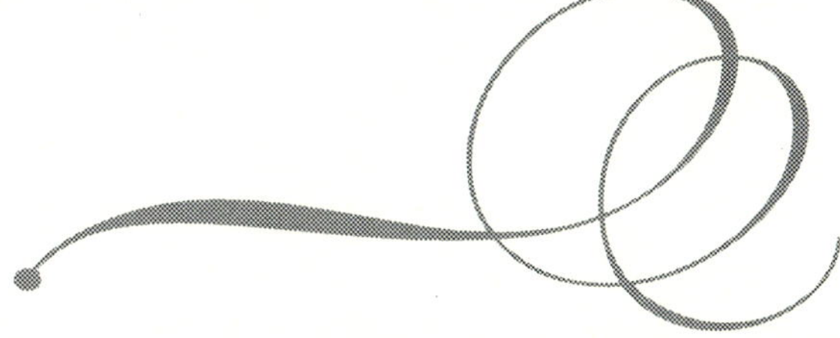

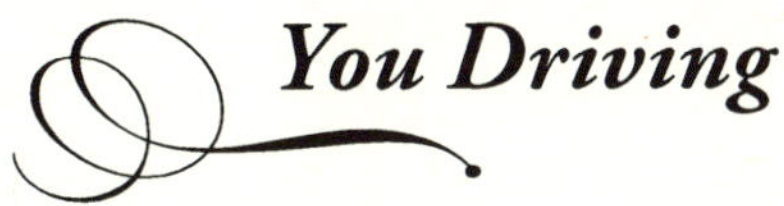

You Driving

This map is cold; its blue and trailing roadside lines
Sprawl across the reds and greens of countrysides
Planted or cropped or rural, or dusted with distant pines
That fret with tiny pinpricks the tops of mountainsides.

But if I think of you in your car, driving by
On roads that swerve or bend to meet the contoured curves
Of fields and farms and rivulets beneath a sky
Hydrangea-hued when the dusk has spread its dry reserves,

That map is warm; your adorable hair, pinned not to blow
In bedraggled frenzy when loopy winds carry it astray,
Stands like a purposive beacon, particularly so
When you're returning, after a personal stay,

To your home and your voice mail, whereupon I'd want
To leave these languorous and overly drawn-out lines.
But I won't because I know their final syllables can't
Be squeezed into your voice mail's impersonal confines.

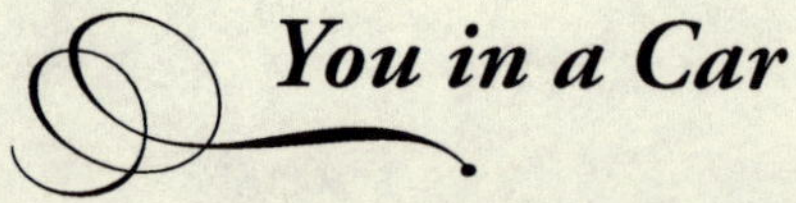

You in a Car

A raving god of murderous movements
Persuaded a child, aged seven or so,
To run from behind a stopped city bus
In front of where we'd intended to go.

Slam! on the brakes went your wonderful foot;
Your lovely arm sprang out to prevent
Your passenger, me, from plummeting forward.
My heartbeats from slow to prestissimo went.

But you stayed quite calm; your beautiful breath
Stayed normal and sane. The child crossed the road.
That god was a god of murderous movements;
You were a goddess who'd thankfully slowed.

Newness

I raged across an oceanic stage,
Complaining how mountains masked the scenic views;
How everything seemed destined to confuse,
And nothing new was ever in *my* news.

But newness is what is glorious in you:
You walk with a timbre totally unique;
The squirrels dart in envy when you tweak
Wild flora from the eddies of your creek.

When you step between your flowered pots
And onto the planks that lead you to *your* earth,
The bird-calls and the frog-peeps volley forth
In sound perpetuations of your worth.

They symbolize the ending of the fight
Between the winter's dark and summer's light.

You and Your Wood Stove

I cannot tell what breezes next will blow
From here to where your wood stove's even glow
Warms your armchair, kitchen, hearth and all.
But I also know I'll soon be in its thrall
To sit and watch while your animals and you
Stir up the air to an irresistible brew

Of fragrant fury, fending off the cold
That soon will lance its way into your fold.
And there I'll sit, surrounded by the smell
Of living cooking heralding all's well,
And feel the stove stave off all winter chills
With a hearty heat that captivates and thrills

My every nerve and sinew, born anew
Because you let me share this warmth with you.

Nature Girl

A black-eyed susan thou art not;
Thine eyes are cornflower-blue.
Laughter to thine eyelids leaps,
And marigolds bestrew
The paths thy sturdy sandals tread
While myrtle leaves and laurel wreaths
Circle thy noble head.

And flowers like the blue forget-me-not
Drive floral pathways through
Fields of mauve and mounded heaps
Of clover free from dew,
Making an earth encarpeted,
Where nature breathes sleepily to thee
A welcome to her bed.

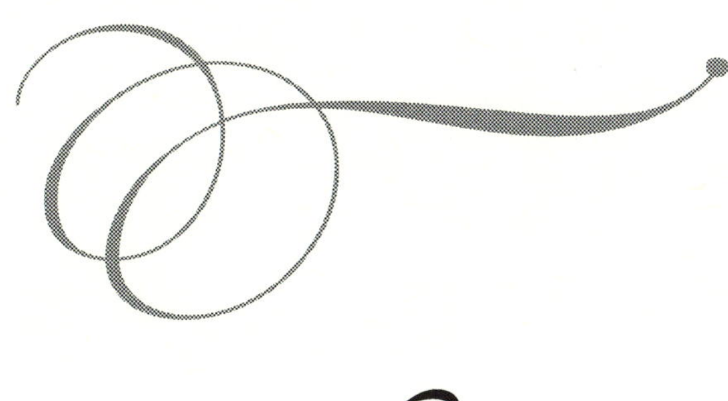

Phone Calls and Letters

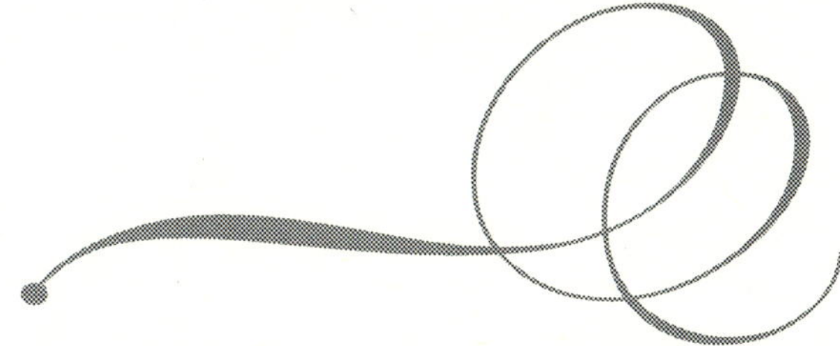

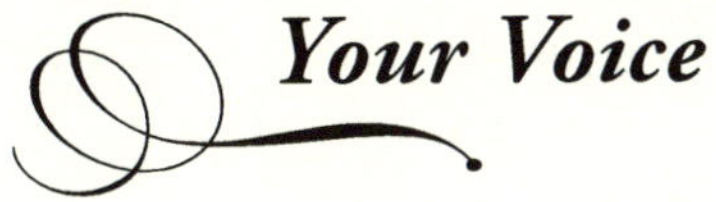

Your Voice

Each day I impatiently await
The sentences and spoken words
You utter from so far away
Into your landline telephone,
And I am dumb with gratitude
To Alexander Graham Bell.

Each night—and often it's quite late—
I eagerly hear the dulcet chords
Of your voice, and thrill to what you say.
I feel a reverence for each tone
You utter with such beatitude
That I can feel it quite dispel

All reservations bred from broody thought.
In your sweet verbal web, I love being caught.

Last Night, You Phoned

Now speaks the world unspeakably to me;
The message is so full, it can't be said.
A simple walk along a street is filled
With something like an ecstasicity
Of streaming zephyrs swarming through my head
While, over me, white clouds hang high that build
On the blue a heaven of childlike light,
While thoughts of you augment my true delight
At having heard you speak to me last night.

I'm tempted to entrap you in my mind;
You, into my full vestigiality
Of verse, fit like perfection into it.
You've been, to my deepest dreams, so closely brought
That I want to wrap you in seamless mists of thought,
A paragon in my wordy web-net caught,
A replica of my dreamed-of Juliet,
A woman with a near-to-mine mentality
Addressed with the warmest words that I can find.

Wooing

SHE:
I slip into your poem. To my delight,
I'm warmest dressed on coolest night.
An ecstasicity in all this wooing—
An elasticity from froing and toing.
What on earth can we be doing?

Whatever it is, I trust it's right
That tongues be still and censure slight,
Since harm to others is not intended;
That no tears be shed or friendship ended;
That we delight in what's extended.

On Reading "Wooing"

"I slip into your poem" stirs my blood;
I feel effusion slip into these lines
At the great golden dream of being with you.
Explosively it bursts, cascading flood,
A wilderness of verses overdue.

You wrote, "I'm warmest dressed on coolest night,"
Evoking for me a golden glimpse of you,
Superlatively slim, walking erect
Across my sunny balcony, upright
With steps not gingerly or circumspect,

To here where I'm standing, rife with pent-up feeling,
Inside my room's dark shade. I entertained
A private joy that you were in my view,
And an instinctive hunch that you're revealing,
Alongside your stride, an undisguised cue

That, were I to shout my feelings to the skies,
You'd try to find a way to harmonise.

Juggling Hens[1]

SHE:
"Now speaks the world
Unspeakably to me."
Thoughts roll unfurled
And hurtle off to thee.
Tongue or pencil? Maybe pens?
Whatever it requires
To juggle words or hens
Till "unspeakable" retires.

[1] She often remarked that our phone calls were like three-ring circuses, ideas bouncing off one another and tearing off on unexpected tangents. She mentioned it to a French-speaking friend of hers with whom this same circus sensation occurred. The friend caught the circus idea, and said, "*Comme les jongleurs de boules* (like juggling balls in the air)." But she heard "Jongleur de poules (juggling hens in the air)" and found the image enchanting.

Voice Mail

This is a poem I can't resist
Reading to you; it has a twist.
Today, in a poem I'd written to you,
Greeting you back from your rendezvous,
I got carried away by your glorious power
To inspire me to verses, hour after hour,
And I wrote in hexameters such a paean
To you that I couldn't come close to seein'
How I'd *not* be cut off by your voice mail machine
For taking too long to convey what I mean.
So I didn't convey it; I sit here, contrite,
And trust that you managed to get back all right.

The Mailbox

SHE:
Our postie slows.
Her motor purrs,
Then turns and goes
With what's now hers
Until next week,
When you will hold
My latest cheek
From pen so bold
That I should dare
To send to poet
Verse so bare
It's sure to blow it.

Now, here's the thing
That bothers me:
Though no mere fling
Our dalliance be,
It feels as though
The bubble's burst
Will leave me low
With unquenched thirst.
Then how shall I
Croak out the words
With throat so dry,
Drowned out by birds?

Enough of this!
It's time to act.
I mustn't miss
What she has stacked
Inside the box
With all the mail.
It won't be socks;
It might be stale.
A word from you?
(Oh, greedy me!)
You see how tough
This thing can be?

So down the ramp
I tread the slope.
Toronto stamp?
Or dashèd hope?
I drop the door—
How truly grand!
On mailbox floor
As if 'twere planned,
An envelope
From you to me!
A cherished hope
Has come to be.

Whither?

SHE:
Whither wouldst thou woo
When once this wooing wanes?
Widely fling thy banner true!
Herald the champion of swains!

Confine not thy gallant's
Gifts to but a single lass.
All damsels crave thy talents
That no man can surpass.

Thine ardour like a rising tide,
Thy will a current flowing,
Tempting me to step aside
Lest I be swept unknowing

To realms beyond my ken,
To air unbreathable to me
Atop a pinnacle-pointed pen,
From which I might not see

Whither next thou wooest
From where I could not cheer
The dame thou next pursuest
Whose colours adorn thy spear.

Canst thou stow the protest's "can't,"
And harken to my plea?
"Thou canst, dear man." That's the chant
Which would do the best for thee.

On Reading "Whither?"

O, you sweet something born from natural earth,
Please do not plague me by saying that your worth
Was overenhanced, extended by my zeal
To crystallize the fondness that I feel.

When pedestals I write, and pinnacles you mention,
They only seem to hide my real intention,
Which is to keep you down to earth, this earth,
This glorious earth where sleep entails rebirth,

And days are growing to romantic nights,
And nothings are transformed to warm delights,
And I am raised by the sight of your natural toes
To kingdoms where I ruthlessly transpose

The natural you to a towering you, hurling at me
Boomerangs of your beautiful poetry.

August 12

SHE:
After we bid each other good-bye,
Wishing each other sweet dreams,
I leased up the dog, and with a sigh,
Stepped into the night's extremes.
The horizon wreathed in clouds quite pale,
The dome above quite dark—
When through Great Dipper swiftly sailed
A brilliant, speeding spark.
A single streak of Perseid shower
Raised me up to fifteen-oh-two,[2]
Where, hand in hand at that late hour,
I lived the event with you.

---

[2] A location.

Reply to "August 12"

A night unchoreographed by shooting stars
And overclouded with a storm's detritus
Has little show on offer to excite us.

And when the moon is missing, and no light shows,
Leaving nothing to see deserving veneration,
And yet the sky had aroused our admiration,

Then fizzle out faint follies of romance;
But your footfall's echo in the hallway of the night
Reminds me of you when the stars maintained their light.

This Particular August

SHE:
Oh, verbal masseur,
How blest am I: before mine eye
The rusted gold and green of field,
The ever-changing sweep of sky,
The thrust of reeds along the ditches,
The bees in goldenrod's sweet riches
Swaying, nodding, caressed by breezes.
Your verbal pampering has revealed
This particular August whose theatre pleases.

Seeing and Hearing

Harken to all the little sparks
That turn the nighttime into day
At the sombre thought you'd change your mind
About keeping me at bay!

Then hear the placid silences
That dot their circles round the guy
Who's caved in to being nice,
Yet never wonders why.

Then see the luscious beauty who
Goes her way, not unaware
Of the spell she casts on throngs of men
Who *have* to stop and stare

At the slippage and wonderful cast of mien
That made her seduce the fugitive me
To adore her, admire her and worship her work,
Ecstatic at feeling so free!

Refusing the Role

SHE:
Am I an active seductress
Setting a thought-out snare
For throngs of men you mention,
Spreading my cosmic hair?

Why does it take a poet,
Celebrating in words,
To make me pause and know it's
Conjecture for the birds?

Do men fancy themselves victims
Of those who catch their eyes?
The rush that often quick comes
To snatch her on the fly?

Not every lass goes fishing
With reel and baited book;
Often she's merely wishing
To frolic in the brook.

Not the fishnet to the water—
Catch-and-hold is not her aim.
Rather the sport than the slaughter;
Rather the dance, the merry game.

So release me from this loathsome role
Of scheming woman with designs
Upon poor, wandering victims' souls,
And let us stay mere valentines.

Blanketed

I lie here writing like a fiend on fire;
You sleep, your misty mass of silken hair
Under your head, which pokes above your blanket,
And you lie asleep, of me unaware.

But I am there indeed, and not too far
From your sleeping body, coiled into a curl
Beneath your blankets; I'm over here
Adjacently, writing about the girl

Lying asleep, her head in misty light
Totally still, hardly breathing, while
I continue writing, with pen on paper,
My praises, in this over-prosey file,

To the lady wrapped in blankets, so darn quiet
That nary a snuffle disturbs my rapturous night.

Decorous Sleep

SHE:
Friday morning at the Holiday Inn.
The steady click and relentless roar
Of air-conditioning's rumbling din
Failed to mask your gentle snore,
A guttural chord so softly purred
By gentle man in decorous sleep.
One more whispered chord I heard.
Only one, then not a peep.

Cataraqui Cemetery Revisited

Oh, you are incorrigible, delicate;
A broad so tough you swear like Sophocles
But tread so gently when you see a bird
That silence spreads a vapour through the trees.

Oh, I recall you interrupting me,
Spouting away on something quite forgotten now,
To show me a bird atop a spreading branch
So big you could not find its name, but knew

He was a hawk, full-fledged with piercing eye.
So I stopped talking and watched it sidle, move
From place to place, now hidden, now in sight,
Until it spread its wings and planed above

Our heads to a branch where you could truly say
It was a red-tailed hawk that *hadn't* flown away.

Retrieval

SHE:
My life is not entirely wasted,
For I have finally tasted
Chez Piggy's sublime peach pie.
And I have walked the hallowed ground
Where red-tailed hawk, without a sound,
Guards a friend who died.

Wake-Up #770[3]

I catch you in a misty morning wake-up.
Easing my way through your fogginess of sleep,
I merge my mind with your quiet and glorious fingers
And pledge affection I shall always keep.

[3] A hotel room number.

Starvation #770

SHE:
All that trouble she takes
To spin her breakfast web
Up on the ceiling above my bed,
Where every wingèd morsel forsakes
The barren controlled atmosphere
Where no fruit flies
Near enough to hear
A hungry spider's cries.

My Printer/Fax Machine

My printer never dares to scoff
If I forget to turn him off,
But yells like murder if I do,
And startles unexpecting you.

Got the Fax

SHE:

[20h 07] Got the fax.
Just the facts, ma'am,
Just the facts—
A jump-out-of-the-skin noise
For heart attacks.
We'll try again, man.
What the hell?
A ding-a-ling, man,
With Old Ma Bell.

[20h 13] Got the fax, all right—
Perhaps all wrong?
But not the man, ma'am.
No murmured delight,
That fax's song.
Call it a night?
Who knows?
He might call back
And prevent another heart attack.

Sounds

The household rackets that I hear
Are all of traffic drawing near,
Or dogs who bark in neighbours' rooms,
Or motorcycles' heady vrooms.

But when alone in reverie
And tummy troubles threaten me,
A breaking wind I can exude,
So quiet that no one thinks I'm rude.

Keen Hearing

SHE:
Yes, poet thou art, and cherished among gallants.
Yet thou displayest additional talents.
Thine ear, old dear, has keenly detected
The slight hint of flatus, though efforts deflected
To right, to left, and partly suppressed.
Talent like this leaves me mighty impressed.

Morning

Through light's varietal facets shines the day,
The day before the day I go away.
And I observe, with gratified surprise,
That it hasn't tried to rain at all this stay.

My raincoat's hanging there, quiet and unused,
And I am quite amazed (and quite enthused)
At how the sun has cast uncensored light
On much that once to me had seemed confused.

Simplicity is the watchword of my dream,
Veracity the emphasis of my theme.
But as the splendid sun rises high today,
It's hope I adopt as entity supreme.

Departure

SHE:
By car, by bus, by train—
You leave, head west today
To shore of lake. You'll stay
Till we shall meet again.

Then train or bus, then car
Will bring you back once more
To where I can explore
Your mind not from afar.

Till then, I'll muddle through
And do the things I must.
Till then, I'll simply trust
In fate and thoughts of you.

Great Wolf Lodge

The Grand Hall

Through the Grand Hall of the Great Wolf Lodge,
Recorded sounds echo of wolves at play
While the Great Father Wolf sends a merciless howl
That chases his rivals further away.

And I am like him, as I pay for the meals
For nine people spending a thrill-packed day
Of swimming and diving and swooping a-down
Through water-tubes flooded with lashings of spray.

And I was like him as I howled at the moon
And chased off the rivals who swarmed round my mate.
And I am like him as I savvily moved
To chase off contenders who swarmed round my gate,

Keeping my den and my lands free for me
And the denizen-guests of my vulpine *famille.*

Wish You Were Here

Long ago I went with my mate and my mother
Through Europe, with the trip including Greece,
Where the devastating depths of the solid mountains
Snared the oracular memories of Delphi,
Locking them fast in the world of Grecian lore.
My mother said she wished my father were with us,
And I remember this now, though I can't recall
The name of any one place seen nearby.

And now, in this contemporary temple,
The Great Wolf Lodge, where children are the gods,
And water splashes its great duets with gravity,
Spraying and spreading itself through the air
Of this warming place for children's fantasies,
I thought, as had my mother, how much I wished
You had been with me; you'd pour your wit
Upon the choppy waves to hear their backchat.

Children, Running

This place has a beauty architectural,
Surprising for a building meant to strike
Into a child a wonder based on stoniness
And wooden logs a child cannot but like.

Here, from my ground-floor corner, I look out
At a morning's sky, more grey than blue, outsplayed
To announce the arrival of a sunny day,
And I see high walls of mighty timber made,

Exteriors redolent of pioneers,
But sheltering a swim-place in excelsis
And clanking machines a-flash with coloured lights
Between which run the children, wild with fancies,

Who thank the world for its modern understanding
Of how a child can find, in a machine,
A something that can lead her on to waxen
Wild about what fun this place has been.

On Visiting a Butterfly Sanctuary

Oh, how I love our near-unspoken thoughts!
Although our words fly like butterflies in all directions,
Function determines where each lands—butterflies whose wings
Are black-and-white all gravitate toward where glass
Is stuffed with blackened wires for local strength, and thus
Offers a black-and-white haven for black-accented wings.
Analogously, words that fly, like heathen fliers
Across the air that separates our heady breaths,
Will fortuitously find natural hiding-forts.
Exotic blacks play strepitoso with the whites,
And the colourful ones, spreading out reds or blues gargantuan,
Will flit between the foliage's greens to alight,
Almost unfelt, on a blazer's facade or a holder's hand,
There to stay until a photograph silently
Shot with the butterfly holding, halted, its wings up in air,
Fixes its picture forever in permanence, just as
You fix what I say, and I fix what you say, in coffers
Of stilled mahogany, cases encrusted forever wherever
The vaults of our minds await the furore of oncoming folly.
Oh, how I love our near-unspoken thoughts!

Heading off to Meet You

Arrangements come, pile up, then go away:
Meals I'm still planning, maybe a taxi fare.
And, packing, I scrabble for places anywhere
To stuff the stuff I'd purchased yesterday.

All these take such a toll on the weary cells
Of my frumpy brain so that when, by the final hour,
Everything's been packed, I'm feeling dour.
All of the work I've done hardly dispels

My premonitions all might not go well.
But then, the packing done, coffee in hand,
With an hour or so to fill before I find
New hospitalities that, I hope, excel

Those I've had, I sit—but with a jolt
Perceive it's tomorrow that we'll meet again.
A moment of trepidation strikes, but then
Pure peace drops on me like a thunderbolt.

Montreal and Kingston

Montreal

I steel my verbal self to ratchet down
Illicitness and everything that could
Betray this incredible meeting-place where we
Have encountered both the beautiful and the good.

For I have seen the sculptures of high towers,
Watched children noisily play in secret groves,
Heard the light tinkle of fork and knife on plate,
And felt the power of everything that moves.

But these all bolster and never compromise
The greater sculpture of your moving form,
Your smile and incredible capture of a light
That brightens every darkness, every storm.

And I, incredulous, across old Montreal,
Feel so appalling-fallen that I crawl
In gratitude for all I know you are.
But though I seem to crawl, I'm standing tall.

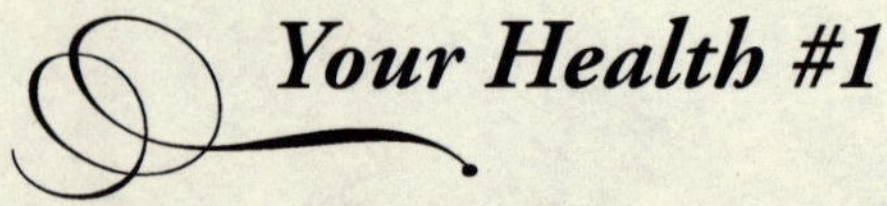

Your Health #1

Oh, damn your physiology:
Its itchy calves, its restless legs,
Its stomach unpredictable
From enteritic dregs.

I want to hold your lovely hand
For longer, but your eyelids droop,
Your breathing slows, and off you drift
Into the void, while I regroup

My bottled forces and concoct
Endless schemes to drown you in
Embraces that you really like,
And poems that simply *can't* begin

Like vapid pastels, but shout out loud
Paeans from your poet proud.

Your Health #2

Grumpelstiltskin never was
The glorious name you now enjoy.
But when I see your morning moods,
That's a name I *could* employ,
As grumpily you fuel your fire,
And feed your creatures till you tire,
And still have breakfast to prepare
For you and me, should I be there.
And all of this because you stretch
Your limber body flat all night,
And then quite justifiably kvetch
Because it takes you time to greet
The morning with the equanimity
Needed to match its gold proximity.

Trappings

Intenser than the waves of solemn sin
That wash the tabled shores of epic tales
Are all the words I want to wrap you in.

And every word is just a metaphor
For what I dream of, trying to begin,
Doting and smooth and reverent, to adore

The wondrous smoothness of your female skin
And fantasise about your being with me.
I do not seek a trap to trap you in,

Although in your clutch I sometimes seem to be,
But still I scarcely dare to entertain
Hopes of a future bright with synchrony

And fine conjunction of your mind with mine,
With nothing forced and nothing faux-divine.

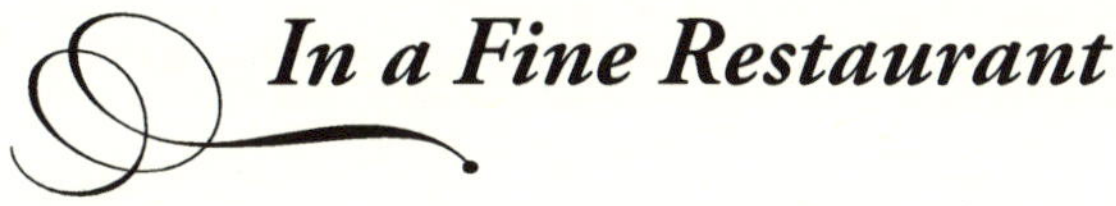

In a Fine Restaurant

I spread these heady words abroad to all:
I know a girl whose solemn majesty
Festively falls on the table that's between
Ourselves and lends me equal dignity.

She has fine pearls about her lustrous neck;
A latticed overblouse of lucid black
Makes her soft chest seem even more alive,
And measures the exquisiteness of her back.

A glass of golden wine winks at her side.
But with her blue-grey eyes, she looks across
The table at where I marvel that she's let
Me bring her here to privilege and gloss.

But later, in the night, I realize
I'll have to keep my head to hold this prize.

Powers

What power I feel with you is not the kind
That olden days called mastery; it's more refined.
I've seen my lovely girlfriend's grey-blue eye
Not turn away from me when I have touched her thigh,

And she's touched mine. Should electricity
Have corkscrewed through our systems? Vivacity
Ran through mine; and through hers I hope I sent
A tiny shred of what I really meant.

A certainty we fit together pervades
My body as I walk her through arcades
And squares to where we'll eat and drink and sit.
But when I see her walk, I must admit

That every move and muscle she displays
Powers me with dreams for days and days and days.

Blue Mountain Resort

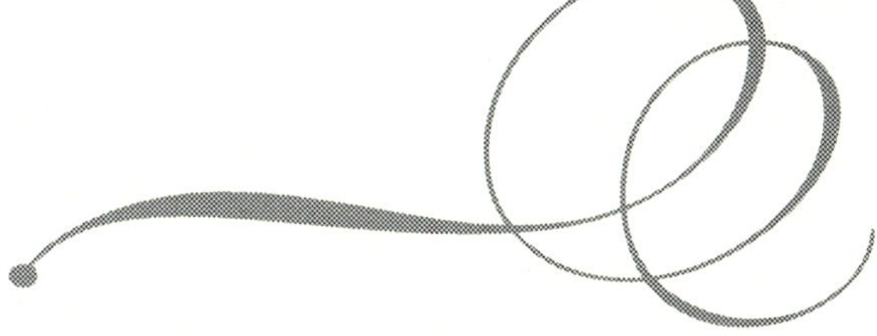

On Getting Soaked Following a Misunderstanding

In sordid junctions of life have I been caught,
And seen my silly follies overwhelm
People with whom I had no argument.
Resolve has entered outgrown disagreements
To set them right, and out of bad, albeit
Accident, has goodness come like paradise
To a whimpering pilgrim plagued with desperation.

And so it was when temperaments united,
Part fury, part instinctive, to enforce
My misadventuring into a rain
That crept to every crevice of our clothing
And into the covert haven of your suitcase,
And reached out arms of penetrating malice.
But at its end, you gloriously smiled
And, distinctive in your womanhood, ironed dry
What had been cold, but now steamed live with warmth.

You as Wedding Guest

Silken-footed, you slowly padded,
Emblem symbolic, clad in blue,
Your way across a noisy crowd
To where I sat awaiting you.

Your slim-hipped walk allowed the fall
Of your dress to repel the unceasing noise
Of the background, and for my eyes alone,
Accentuated your walk and pace and poise.

And so, O heroine who had been
Bred by field and forest and fen,
I watched you cross that noisy crowd
Like a lynx or a leopard to share the den

To which I walked with you thereafter,
A glittering bird in a teal-blue dress,
Dazzling in the dark and cold—
An Aphrodite, nothing less.

Temptation Resisted

On your side you lie, but the violinic curve
Of your waist and the rising of your hipline's swell
Seemed to my eyes so lovely as to compel
Me to want to picture it without reserve.

And seeing that curve in the dark, with just a light
From another room exposing your silhouette,
I wished for a moment simply to forget
All niceties and hold you warm and tight.

But then a subtle noise, some snuffling sighs
Arose from you as you slept, and so I brought
My roaming arm back to my side and thought
How the curve of your waist had charmed my roaming eyes.

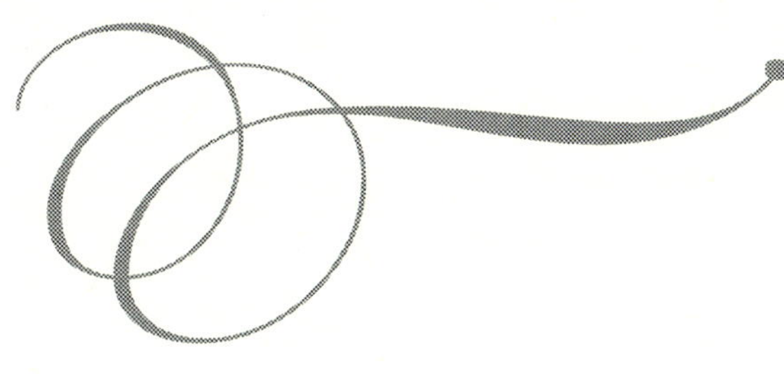

Praise Poems

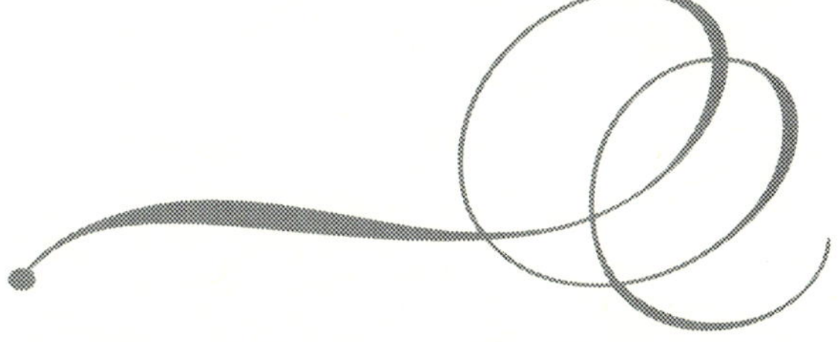

Endnote #1

Although my death is drawing nearer,
My life to me is more divine
Than ever it was in my youth time's years,
When I was plotting, sad but benign,
How to woo a woman's mind.
Life was indecorous; it was a grind.

But life for me is now much dearer,
Now that your path is crossing mine,
Than ever it was when, plagued with fears
And rages, I had crossed the line
From gentleman to boor. But you
Filter what's bitter from my brew.

Endnote #2

Question: “I welcome old age with open arms
Because it brings me nearer death.”
How shall I read this when happiness
Brightens my eye and burns my breath?

Answer: I wrote those lines when mortified
By one whom I suspect has died.
But now they are no longer true,
Nor can they be while I’m with you.

Hair

How lovely your comet, cosmic hair
Looks as it hangs in a sweet percussion
Of flurried strands against your cushion
Of shoulders smooth and pink and bare!

Oh, to be a molecule
Tangled in hairs that, unable to stay
Apart from each other, checked its way
Into and out of a world of misrule.

Oh, wind up the music to overloud—
The better to chorus your lack of coiffure,
The better to prove that you, paramour,
Of your natural beauty cannot be too proud.

But I must not lose myself in your hair;
Some would say I was mad—poet, beware!

Death and Love

La mort deprives us of we know not what.
L'amour provides us with everything we've got.

Nightingale

No nightingale has ever known
The affection human beings have shown
To each other in song or rhyme or dance—
Melodies merging to forge romance.

For many a peasant or doughty knight
In days of yore had sung out in the night,
From the wall of a fort or the shade of a glade,
His clamourings for an amorous maid.

And now, even now, the air-waves roar
With the tinkles of texting and many a score
Of entreatings, enticings, and very much more
In the chase for a somebody unsought before.

So here I write testaments of desire
And gild my words till they aspire
To beat the nightingale at his game,
And sing to you songs that are never the same.

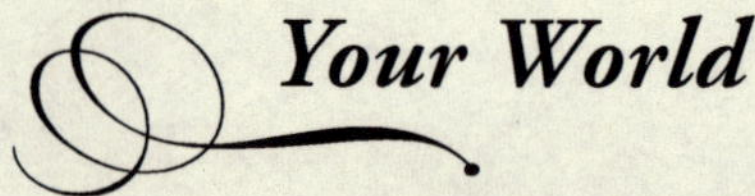

Your World

I want to curse realities that conspire
To keep me from attending more to you
Than to courtesy or duty, and that fire
Anger at needless delays to be worked through.

So I put you on a plateau where pure bliss
Shields you from the day of the daily grind;
I put you on a map of paradise
Extending to every corner of my mind.

I put you in a dreamwork where my brain
Sends you to estates of bucolic glow;
Where your sentinel self waits, warden, for the grain
My eager self for you expects to grow.

O, you enchanting, unbelievable girl,
You whizz my poor sensorium to a whirl!

Feeding You

I'll feed you with frantic poems like the demon that I am;
Into your eager mouth, sonnet-snippets shall I cram.
Between your lovely teeth, the softest sweetest verse I'll place,
And reverential odes your smooth and waiting taste buds grace.

"Food for the gods" with golden music will be blended,
And honeys and meads and nectars with verse will be distended
Till their powers satiric, soporific, sating will be blown
To corners of your tongue that you'd find you'd never known.

But here I stumble, for if I go further with this, I'll be
Tempted like blazes to wander into some chicanery
In which, like a schoolboy, I'll pretend that food is just a ploy
To get into deeper detail about the things I would enjoy

If left alone to feast with you. So I humbly take my leave,
Knowing that, from harassment, no artist can get reprieve.

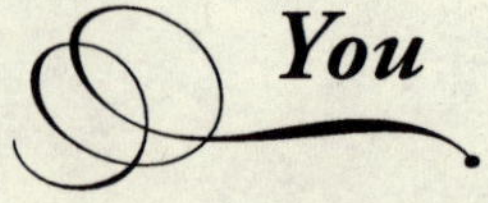

You

You're an impossible girl who won't go away.
Wherever I stir or move, whatever the day,
Whatever the weather, whatever the duties I do,
I'm thinking of you; wherever I'm looking for you,
You're there, resplendent—you, you, you.
I adore you so much, all I'd be able to do
Would be to burble repeatedly, "You, you, you,"
If somehow, somewhere, you were no longer you.

There, that's out; my pen can slower run
And pinion into infinities all I've done
To make me search every sensation I'm in
For the you whom I yearn to engage in my sin
Of effulgent indulgence in engorging you
With all the outrageousness I can brew
To replenish the ravishing you, you, you,
And no how, nowhere, would you not be you.

Confession

As one who's loved, and often loved too well,
I know with what abandon I can write,
Even to women I hardly know at all—
Sweet nothings on a starry wall of night.

But I cannot "with abandon" write to you
Emptiness sandwiched into verse.
You know my mind so well you'd see right through
Hypocrisy, philandering, or worse.

Only what's honest (given more or less
"Poetic license" to exaggerate!)
Is what I offer you. But I confess
That, knowing your sensitivity to be great,

I sometimes hold back and keep a silent tongue
On wishes some people might castigate as wrong.

Joy

"Idle" is not a name for joy; neither is
"Sporadic" or "spontaneous" or "sudden."
Joy has no name, and so it cannot speak;
All it can do is laugh or cry at its truth.

And laughing or crying is all there really is
In joy; my own joy came, unbidden,
From an unbridled furlough of a week
When you rekindled embers from my youth.

Your Higher Power #1

O, you inchoate darling, how I sigh
For the coming days to be cornucopia
Where the coruscations of your lovely brain
Turn every day to a holiday again.

And though high winds may dash and thunder round,
Driving my dafter dreamings underground,
I nonetheless ask you (and, perhaps, your higher power)
To please let me love you hour after hour after hour.

Your Higher Power #2

I have no need of shifting skies to know
That the only heaven above the clouds that go
Sideways all day across their static blue
Is one that is a higher power to you.

And when you gaze intensely at the sky,
Wondering if that power has passed you by,
Please know that I stand behind you, always ready
To catch you if you start to feel unsteady.

Injustices

I flee injustices, or try to fight them,
But no injustice do I deem it when
I fantasise imaginary versions
Of clinch romantic between us now and then.
Injustices for me would be coercions

Forced on your resistances despite them;
The only wantonness that I'd want
Is wantonness that you'd truly like,
And then injustices I'd truly taunt
By telling them to go and take a hike.

Paean

O, beloved, dressed in black and beauty,
Hide not thy proud and wisdom-loving waist,
Nor the fine intimations of thy talk,
Nor the accoutrements that always graced
Thy winsome outer ways and winning walk.

O, beloved, dressed in beauteous black,
Hide not the waist I want to claim and hold,
But let me look at it, admire it and admit,
Just as my early fancies had foretold,
How happy my arms would be to circle it.

Solar Flares

Solar flares of magnanimity
Resemble my fervent wallowings of content
That you've been moved to set your eyes on me
And taught me what true admiration meant.

You are so lovely yet so wise in look
That you appear to assess all incidents
As artworks spread across deep veins of time—
Potential wonders swathed in eloquence.

And your hair is cut and cropped, but even yet
Is wild enough soft wisplets to release.
It says that you are infinitely lovable;
You radiate war that is at peace with peace.

A Collage of Various Clothes

Your silken robe shows off your stately head
As loosely over you its silk is led.
Your yellow T-shirt smoothly, tightly drapes
The pillars of your lovely shoulders' shapes.
Your string of pearls invites, inveigles, in
Idolatry of your neck's exquisite skin.
The tremulous softness of your longest gown
Falls, in a lavender splendour, freefall down
Your velvet back and dorsal curves to find
And cover legs by goddesses designed.
And seemingly fitted to your feet from birth,
Your sandals match the groundswell of the earth.
But the acme and peak of all that you possess
Are eyes that reflect your strength and tenderness.

Vanity's Virtue

I think, in a fight, she could beat me;
She's almost as tall as me.
Being faster, she'd maybe defeat me,
And she's younger, her movements more free.

But fighting a woman is never
Instilled in a fighting man's blood.
It's fighting *for* women that's clever;
It's fighting bad men that is good;

So sometimes a man meets a woman
For whom he feels more than desire.
He wants her to know that he's human;
He wants her to know he's no liar.

He dreads she respond with disdain;
He shows her he's working for her.
He hopes he can free her from pain,
For neither want pain to recur.

And so, with a vanity's virtue,
He tries to ensure she can sleep
By insisting that "I'll never hurt you"
Or give her occasion to weep.

But all the time he knows,
Deep in his innermost heart,
That women don't like to disclose
They're unhappy at playing that part.

So I'll show my poetic intentions,
Ecstatic, subversive, or rude,
Blanketing all my pretensions
To be something other than crude.

Your Photo #1

Your photo brings your strength of youth
To nowadays, when you still look strong;
A sort of firmness in your mouth
Suggests my verdict isn't wrong.

For strength comes from an armature
Inside a sculpture, smooth and free,
And when I see your portraiture,
And think you spare some strength for me,

I want to flop (a metaphor),
But don't because I might be right
To fear I turn you off before
Your strength has melded with the might

My steadfast brain can still endow
Upon the you I'm seeing now.

Your Photo #2

You're featured as a patron of the arts
In an article whose photo shows your face
As parable whose vitality imparts
Vainglory to a lad like me, who starts
To be refired by your loveliness and grace.

And patron of the arts you are, as such,
But even more you're patroness of me.
How could I write so desperately much
Were I not hungry for the sound and touch
Of you, whose photo shines resplendently?

Your photo sends me cartwheels to my brain;
I reel, and I recover, from its sight.
I ponder your image time and time again,
And when poor daylight starts to fade and wane,
Your photo heralds all the wealth of night.

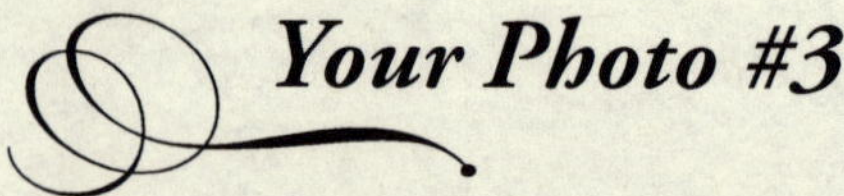

Your Photo #3

I want to have no force to barricade
Myself from waxing crazy over you;
I love to see your photograph displayed
Where I can proudly graze thereon and chew

Your femaleness entrappèd in a wealth
Of strength and beauty I want to savour here.
I want to taste its force and steady stealth;
I never, ever want it to disappear.

I want to immerse myself, engorge my fill
Of all that your photo's premises foretell.
I want to relish your photo's beauty till
Reality breaks its earthly heaven's spell.

And I want to cherish its truth: as time goes by,
Though your photo fades, it can never tell a lie.

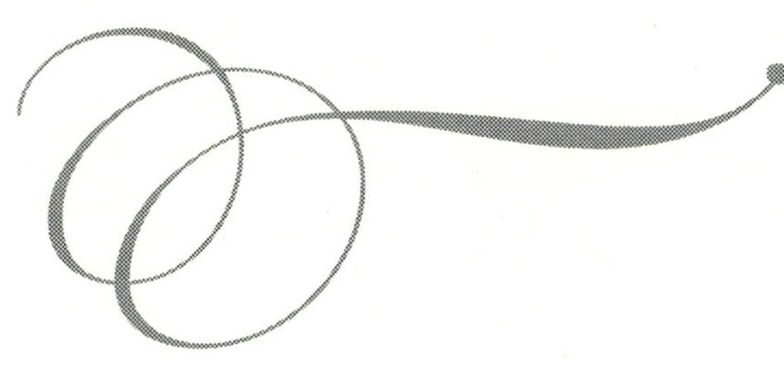

Sleep Poems

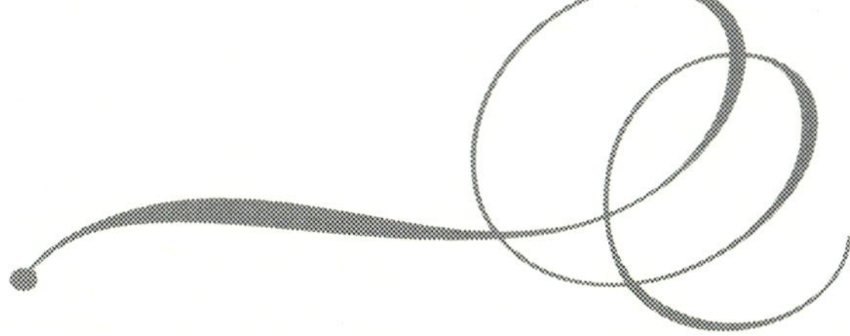

Your Gown #1

You, in a dull grey gown that speaks of night,
Routinely rob the stars of all their powers.
What years could take, you did in petty hours
To fling the stone that put my grief to flight.

And should the dawn of a new oncoming day
Darken the east with cloud-shafts of despair,
You, in your garb of dullest grey, are there
To charm its madcap storminess away.

And when the day closes into dusk of eve,
Sybil- or Cassandra-like, you stand,
Refusing to let apathy gain an upper hand
As I stave off a tendency to grieve.

Oh, how I envy that flowing, sombre gown
That folds you in its drabness from your shoulders down!

My Verbal Pampering

Now I would pamper thee to dreamful sleep,
And waft gold stardrops near thy closing eyes,
The easier thy tryst with dreams to keep.

And when, in the dark, thy mind greets their foray,
Thy consciousness to meet and tranquillize,
Let thyself, on their stardrops' gold, be wafted away.

Signing Off

"May garland-birds drop heaven on your head."
These were my final words to send you to your bed.

Your Gown #2

As you lie asleep with your gown of softest grey,
I see again how your head has a noble shape.
I can envisage angels in the night
Hovering and jostling to lean and peer
At you, to them an angel in disguise.

And I can see them pulling slightly away.
Tempted to take up blankets to redrape
Your sleeping self with covers lying so light
And yet so heavy that you disappear,
Buried in slumber, even from angels' eyes.

Now Is the Time

Now is the time for sleep to hold your hand,
And slumber to caress your sleeping hair.
I play a role protective, so I stand
Here, where I watch you sleeping over there,
And oh how I want to take the place of sleep
And hold your perfect hand till peace appears,
And slumber yields to me and lets me keep
You warm and safe for years and years and years.

Watching You Sleep

Full silence reigned while I wrote the poem above,
But now a tiny sigh betrays your move—
Not to awaken, but perhaps to dreaming
That what one wants need not be idle seeming.

I want you to want the things that I want too.
I want each morning's light to seem to you
Evidence of a future filled with light
Where everything we do just seems, well, right.

You, Fast Asleep

If ever your sleep were passionate, content,
And you strained yourself toward a dreamed-of sun,
Moonlight from unconsciousness would be sent

To keep you still, so very fast asleep
That any aspiring watcher would be bent
On asking why your slumber was so deep.

And, likewise, were *I* selfishly to inspect
Your cheeks to see if secretly you weep
Despite the random lashings of respect

I lavish on your self when you're awake,
And find, to my relief, no hint of tears,
I'll positively treasure my mistake.

But I'd spied on you, or so it would appear!
Even in poems, the ethics must be clear.

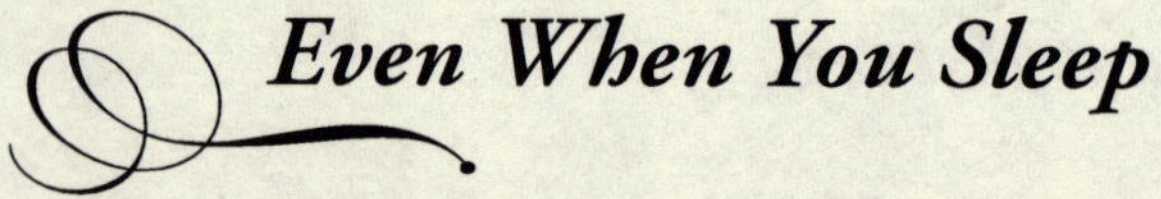

Even When You Sleep

If I have hurt you in some subtle way,
By lack of caution in the things I say,
Please know that a residue of loss and want
Has made me overeager in my hunt
For someone I'll want to cherish every day.

But now I've found that someone: you. Your speech,
Your nature knowledge that you love to teach,
Your fascination when we're volubly talking
Of music or art or stocks or food or walking,
Enable me to hope I'll never breach

Promises, already made in verse, to keep
You safe but free, even when you sleep.

To Sleep I Want to Go

And now to sleep I want to go.
But oh! you are not there!
Where you slept is emptiness,
A vacant slice of air.

And where the rising hummock of your thigh
Rose to attend the nuptials of the night,
Now there is nothing but an empty space
Dark in the darkness, sheer nothing in the light.

You, Asleep

A gentle breath, a gentle sigh
Draws me close to where you lie.
I look at you and ache to see
The radiance of your symmetry.
And so I move myself away
So quick and quiet, one might say
I'm camouflaging, for your sake—
A rude desire to watch you wake.

Going to Sleep

You said you owned a gown with woven crabs
Sidling around its ample hem.
Nothing they'd know of the beauty of its wearer;
Being brainless, there's no knowledge they could claim.

So if I were there as you wandered off to bed,
And noticed those crabs a-lilting with each step,
I'd know they knew nothing of how you looked
Softly walking your way to gentle sleep.

And so, uncluttered by envy or distress
Of the kind a human rival might bestow
On my doting brain while I silently observed
Your hemline as you padded quietly through

The growing darkness to your waiting bed,
I'm glad those crabs were not alive, but dead.

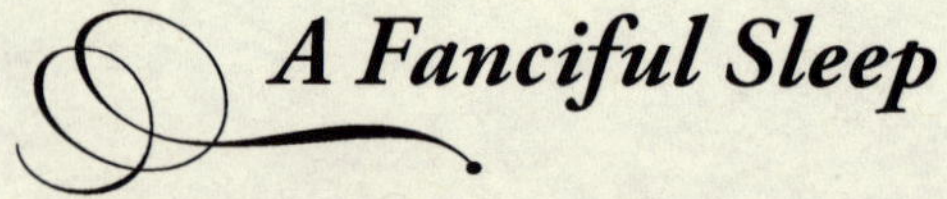

A Fanciful Sleep

A fanciful sleep can make us toss and turn,
Making you wonder what we'd done to earn
Such restlessness that it aches.

A dreamy sleep can make us soft and yielding,
Making us ask what treasure it is we're shielding
That all our composure shakes.

But a sleep in which our eyelids close fast-shut,
And nothingness pervades us, is a cut
Less tremulous.

It means the dimming memories of today
Put down their tools and idly walk away
From irritating us.

It means the sobering thinkings of tomorrow,
With all they may forebode of future sorrow,
Are laid to solemn rest.

And if I see you sleep that kind of sleep,
I'll know your slumber is so very deep
We'll both feel blessed.

Thousands

A thousand-threaded count of a nighttime sheet
Sounds neat,
But after it's been washed and folded for weeks,
It breaks.

A thousand random ripplings in your hair
Linger there;
Even when nighttime steals the hours away,
They stay.

May a thousand pleasant dreamings fill your sleep
And softly keep
You free from fears and worries in the night
Until it's light.